the POEMS

Paulina –
May all your interpretations in life
empower you!

Blair Smith
ThePoems
LVI7B

BLAIR SMITH

Printed in the United States of America

ISBN-13: 9781723882456

10 9 8 7 6 5 4 3 2

EMPIRE PUBLISHING
www.empirebookpublishing.com

Chief Editors: Dennis Smith and Clark Smith

To my family:
You are my everything.
You inspire me.

To my readers:
I am honored you are holding this book.
"May all your interpretations in life empower you."

-Blair Smith

EARLY ENDORSEMENTS

"The author evokes and touches on many aspects of the human spirit from the *nothingness* to the *all-encompassing connection to everything*. A rare and inspiring creative collection."

-Jorge Haddock, San Juan, Puerto Rico
President, University of Puerto Rico

"Through his poetry, Blair Smith takes the human condition and strips it bare, leaving us vulnerable and requiring us to question our purpose. He leads us to a place of inspiration, possibilities and hope. Read *The Poems* and you will feel challenged and empowered to make a difference in your personal life and in the world around you. "

-Scott W. Murdock, Sanur, Bali
Captain, United States Navy (Retired)

"It takes courage to write poetry. This work has searched for uneasy answers, doubted accepted beliefs, and expressed uncharted feelings. Take the time to read these poems if you are willing to join the author on these complicated journeys."

-Dr. Gloria E. Bader, San Diego, CA
Founder of The Bader Group

"This author was once a warrior defending a nation, here you gain a moving introspection into the caring heart and perceptive mind that drives him. Now with inspiring wisdom expressed so lucidly here, his work is ours forever."

-Robert (Coach) Cunningham, Las Vegas, NV
Colonel, United States Air Force (Retired)

"*The Poems* is a beautiful embodiment of Blair's transformational journey as a student and then as a coach of ChoiceCenter's EQ Leadership trainings. By exploring the power of vulnerability, living in the present moment, and being in service to all people, Blair inspires us all to move in love everyday towards a world that works."

-Robyn A. Williams, Las Vegas, NV
Founder and CEO of Choice Center Leadership University

"I met the author during one of the most vulnerable times in my life, his gentle and firm life coaching supported me to crack the code to the powerful gift of forgiveness. His poetry reveals that raw, real, uncomplicated heart of gold that he possesses. I have the honor to know this human personally and you are fortunate to know him through his poetry."

-Dr. Susana Acevedo, Lafayette, CA
Medical Doctor

"A relatively young man, Blair Smith harvests every breathing moment with little regard to age, climate, geography, or circumstance. He sucks all juice from the fruit; he extracts all marrow from each and every bone. Said another way, he chews, swallows, and digests his temporal passage better than any being I know. And now, by grace, those gifts (*The Poems*) are shared with us."

-Terrence M. Doyle, Alexandria, VA
Policy Lead, National Nuclear Security Administration

"*The Poems* by Blair Smith has shown us it is indeed possible to traverse the intensity of life's dramatic peaks and valleys while having the ability to reach within and create your own nirvana. Through his sincere and authentic writing, it is easy to see the beauty that runs deep and I am thrilled that he has an opportunity to share his passion with the world."

-Karen Brasch, San Diego, CA
Principal Technical Program Manager, Intuit

"This great collection of wisdom and irony challenges us to question our beliefs, to talk about what we are for instead of what we are against. To embrace the positive, reject the negative and abandon certainties."

-Joe Keith, Medford, OR
President, Million Air

"*The Poems* contains deep thinking, intensity and wit. This book breaks stereotypes and creates new paradigms, while finding beauty in forgiveness, joy in giving back, and values the impact of helping others less fortunate. This book will inspire, challenge, and help any reader to reflect as they write and reflect on their own story."

-Robb Schwartz, MBA, MHROD, Orange, CA
Senior Project Manager, Boeing Aircraft, Retired

"This is the poetry of a man looking at the fullness of life. The words, thoughts and reference points reach out to explore this journey and his place within it. It's a song of praise and a pledge to keep learning and growing and contributing; its rare insight into the emotional life of a complex man."

-Deborah Stone, San Diego, CA
Executive Assistant

"If you have ever wondered about things you were taught, things you have read, or things you have heard, this book will speak to you. I am positive that there is something in here for every person. Be brave and find that something which is for you.

After reading his poems, I see that the author is one of those rare beings who truly immerses himself in the process of life. I also see that my nervousness in reading *The Poems* was solely related to my own failure to delve into my own shortcomings and my own heavy baggage. I defy anyone to read these poems and not be touched in some way. Take a breath, step off the safety platform and read this book."

-Joan Holland Day, Casa Grande, AZ
Retired Social Worker

FORWARD

These free verse "poems" do not follow the traditional requirements of rhyme and meter. My sense is that, in the end, content surpasses form. Initially, my intent was to create a "thought heirloom" for my children and their progeny in the hope that future family souls I may never meet or know might at least know me through my writings. Early on, I started sharing "the poems" with my brother Clark and then, with his encouragement, began to share them with my wife and super kids, Kiera, Jake, and Trent. Then, thanks to their positive reaction, I took a leap of faith and posted a few on Facebook and sent a wider sample to close friends. Once again, I was encouraged by positive feedback all around which led me to broaden my thoughts to include publishing "the poems" for general consumption. Thank you in advance for reading them. I sincerely hope you take away a thought or two that will add to your life.

Recurring themes include the folly of "Human Certainty" and my urge to always keep questioning; the absolute need for inner balance brought by continual cultivation of "Emotional Intelligence"; the human disregard for and rape of "Mother Earth" and the urgency to heal our womb of life; and, occasional "Sprinklings of Humor" and "Irony" for after all, man has proven to be both funny haha and funny peculiar.

-Blair Smith

Table of Contents

FORWARD i

CHAPTER 1 1

EMOTIONAL INTELLIGENCE 1

NOTHING 3

BEING IN SERVICE 5

THE DEPTH OF FORGIVENESS 9

RISK IT 13

LIMITING BELIEFS 17

GAINING ALTITUDE 21

THE LAW OF ATTRACTION 25

CONSERVATION OF THOUGHT 29

THE CLIMB 31

THE BALANCE 33

BLANK CANVAS 35

THE VAST STILLNESS 39

QUESTIONING DUALITY 41

QUESTION 43

WAKING THOUGHTS 45

VULNERABILITY 47

SALIENT QUOTES 51

CHAPTER 2 55

HUMAN CERTAINTY 55

CERTAINTY VERSUS THE FOX 57

WHY DO WE BELIEVE WHAT WE BELIEVE 59

HUMAN BELIEF: THE DARK SIDE OF THE HUMAN MIND 63

THE CRUCIAL QUESTION 65

HOPE VERSUS THE ZEALOT 67

NEW SCRIPTURE 69

SALIENT QUOTES...71

CHAPTER 3 73

MANKIND 73

I WONDER...75

SKEWED RELATIVITY 77

THE HUMAN MIND 79

HOPE 81

COMMON DENOMINATOR 83

THE TRUTH OF THE MATTTER 85

CONDITIONED RESPONSE.................................87

MANKIND 89

MAN'S NATURE...91

SALIENT QUOTES...93

CHAPTER 4 95

MOTHER EARTH 95

COMMENT FROM THE EARTH 97

ABSURDITY...99

LAMENT..101

CHIEF SEATTLE SOUNDED WARNING 103

COFFEE WITH CHIEF SEATTLE 105

THE CANYON TRAIL 109

BATHROOM MANNERS 111

ONE DAWN ATOP HALEAKALA 113

GIGI's SONG 115

SEARCH 119

THE ULTIMATE OBSCENITY 123

SALIENT QUOTES..125

CHAPTER 5 127

THE CREATIVE POEMS...127

THE RIVER SOUL 129

Background Reading on Operation Babylift 131

OPERATION BABYLIFT...133

CRITERION 135

BIRD WORDS...137

OMAR SPEAKS AGAIN 139

MODERN TRESPASSING 141

THE FACE OF PRIDE 143

A PUZZLE SOLVED 147

THE MIRROR 149

I AM 151

SALIENT QUOTES..153

AFTERTHOUGHT 159

ABOUT THE AUTHOR 161

ACKNOWLEDGEMENTS.......................................163

AVAILABILITY 175

ELEGY 176

the POEMS

CHAPTER 1

EMOTIONAL INTELLIGENCE

"You must be the change you wish to see in the world." - *Gandhi*

"The Golden Rule is of no use to you whatever unless you realize it's always your move." - *Frank Crane*

… denn da istkeineStelle,
die dich nichtsieht. Du musstdeinLebenandern.
(… for there is no place that does not see you.
You must change your life.) - *Rainer Maria Rilke*

"Impossible is just a big word thrown around by small men who find it easier to live in the world they have been given than to explore the power they have to change it. Impossible is not a fact. It's an opinion. Impossible is not a declaration. It is a dare. Impossible is potential. Impossible is temporary. Impossible is nothing."
-Muhammad Ali

"One Moment in Annihilation's Waste
One moment, of the Well of Life to taste -
The Stars are setting, and the Caravan
Starts for the dawn of Nothing - Oh, make haste!"
-Omar Khayyam

NOTHING

There is a great freedom in coming from nothing

    free from attachments, free from circumstance

    free from definition, free from our past

    no words, no labels can get to us

    unless we come from something

    unless we are attached

Coming from nothing is a shield

    against critics, against self

    the past is gone forever, the future not here

    only the present moment exists

    there are infinite possibilities in the present moment

    if we come from nothing

Surrendering the past ends resistance,

    attachment and circumstance

    Surrendering to nothing creates possibility

    Only then is there free movement

    within which to create

    I choose to come from nothing

Why do we assign meaning to our attachments?

    I'm starting to get that there is nothing to get

    I'm becoming satisfied with not being satisfied

    Just as I'm satisfied, I am not satisfied again

    There is really nothing to get

    when you are attached to nothing,

    nothing can get to you.

Dedicated to my friend Jorge Haddock.... because it means nothing!

"We never reflect how pleasant it is to ask for nothing." *-Seneca*

"What is life? It is the flash of a firefly in the night. It is the breath of a buffalo in the wintertime. It is the little shadow which runs across the grass and loses itself in the sunset."
-Crowfoot, Blackfoot warrior and orator, 1890

"The heart has its reasons of which reason knows nothing."
-Blaise Pascal

"I believe in nothing, everything is sacred.
I believe in everything, nothing is sacred."
-Tom Robbins, Even Cowgirls Get the Blues

BEING IN SERVICE

It is in giving
> that we receive

And the more we give
> the more we receive

Some are afraid to feel
> how powerful they really are

And the catalyst they can be for others
> to feel equally empowered

To feel true power
> one needs to be in service

The cup only over flows
> when we receive back
> more than what we have given away

In serving others
> we not only assist another person's well being
> we also bless ourselves

Making a difference in someone else's life

spurs us to make greater efforts

to serve even more

As servants

our time is not always our own

intention is all

Dedicated to Terrence (Touchdown) Doyle, a man for others.

Author's note: When you are in service you really don't need feedback from others because the act itself makes us feel good about ourselves and the difference made for others. We can continue to live self-centered lives, but when we are in service to others is when the magic happens.

Simply stated, serving others makes us happy. Studies demonstrate that helping others ignites our own happiness. Researchers at the London School of Economics explained the relationship between volunteering and happiness in a large group of American adults and discovered that the more people volunteer, the happier they become. A summary of their findings was published in the journal Social Science & Medicine that concluded, "Compared with people who never volunteered, the odds of being very happy rose 7 percent among those who volunteer monthly and 12 percent for people who volunteer every 2-4 weeks. Among weekly volunteers, 16 percent felt very happy – a hike in happiness comparable to having an income of $75,000-$100,000 versus $20,000." In other words, serving others will give people a happiness boost comparable to moving from poverty to the middle-class." As Mother Teresa reminds us, we are all Jesus in distressing disguise.

"The best way to find yourself is to lose yourself in the service of others." -*Mahatma Gandhi*

"Give and it will be given to you." -*Jesus Christ*

"Every man is guilty of the good he did not do." -*Voltaire*

"The life of a man consists not in seeing visions and in dreaming dreams, but in active charity and in willing service." -*Henry Wadsworth Longfellow*

"Every day, people serve their neighbors and our nation in many different ways, from helping a child learn and easing the loneliness of those without a family to defending our freedom overseas. It is in this spirit of dedication to others and to our country that I believe service should be broadly and deeply encouraged." -*John McCain*

"The end of all knowledge should be service to others." -*Cesar Chavez*

"The highest of distinctions is service to others." -*King George VI*

"I've learned that people will forget what you said, people will forget what you did, but people will never forget how you made them feel." -*Maya Angelou*

"We are all here on earth to help others; what on earth the others are here for I don't know." -*W. H. Auden*

THE DEPTH OF FORGIVENESS

Why is forgiving others so hard?

Is it this?

The depth of forgiveness
    is forgiveness of self
    for hanging onto
    our need to be right
    about our stories, and hard circumstances

Fear of being wrong
    about our stories
    challenges who we think we are
    as defined by past experiences
    preventing the power of now

Having the power to forgive
    and not exercising the power to forgive
    jails the finer human spirit
    Setting free the forgiver
    and the forgiven

Exercising your power to forgive

reveals the power

to create new

human beings

as creators in and of the moment

Dedicated to my friend Susana Acevedo and all those who need to find the absolute freedom of forgiveness.

Author's note: Who do you need to forgive to forgive yourself?

"The weak can never forgive. Forgiveness is the attribute of the strong." -*Mahatma Gandhi*

"The practice of forgiveness is our most important contribution toward the healing of the world." -*Marianne Williamson*

"To forgive is to set a prisoner free and discover the prisoner was you." -*Lewis B. Swedes*

"When you forgive you in no way change the past, but you sure do change the future." -*Bernard Meltzer*

"There is no forgiveness in nature." -*Hugo Betti*

"Forgiveness is the fragrance that the violet sheds on the heel that has crushed it." -*Mark Twain*

"Forgiveness is the final form of love." -*Reinhold Niebuhr*

"It is easier to forgive an enemy that to forgive a friend." -*William Blake*

"When a deep injury is done, we never recover until we forgive."
-Alan Paton

"Always forgive your enemies - nothing annoys them so much."
-Oscar Wilde

"God will forgive me it's his job." *-Heinrich Heine*

RISK IT

To know victory

    we risk defeat

To conquer self

    we risk facing fears

To love with all your heart

    we risk being vulnerable

    like saying "I love you" first

    without expectation of hearing it back

To feel our true power

    we risk knowing our weakness

To change our relationship with risk

    we change our relationship with self

To leap off the cliff

    we learn to fly

To realize it is always your turn

to go first

to be vulnerable

to risk it all

to have it all

Dedicated to Karen Brasch who has learned it is always her turn to go first.

"You miss one hundred percent of the shots you do not take."
-Michael Jordan

"Rules are made for people who aren't willing to make up their own." *-Chuck Yeager*

"Only those who will risk going too far can possibly find out how far one can go." *-T.S. Elliott*

"He who is not courageous enough to take risks will accomplish nothing in life." *-Muhammad Ali*

"The biggest risk is not taking a risk....In a world that is changing really quickly, the only strategy that is guaranteed to fail is not taking risks." *-Mark Zuckerberg*

"Jump, and you will find out how to unfold your wings as you fall." *-Ray Bradbury*

"You have to take risks. We will only understand the miracle of life fully when we allow the unexpected to happen."
-*Paolo Cuelho*

"Be brave. Take risks. Nothing can substitute experience."
-*Paolo Cuelho*

"If you take no risks you suffer no defeats. But if you take no risks, you win no victories." -*Richard M. Nixon*

"Take risks. Ask big questions. If you don't make mistakes you're not reaching far enough." -*David Packard*

"If no one ever took risks, Michelangelo would have painted the Sistine floor." -*Neil Simon*

"Many will call me an adventurer, and that I am, only one of a different sort: one of those who risks his skin to prove his platitudes." -*Che Guevara*

"Take calculated risks. That is quite different from being rash."
-*George S. Patton*

"There are lots of risks, but without risks there is no reward. I think the reward is bigger than the risk." -*Brock Lesnar*

"If no pain, then no love. If no darkness, no light. If no risk, then no reward. It's all or nothing. In this damn world, it's all or nothing." -*Glennon Doyle Melton*

"Once we believe in ourselves, we can risk curiosity, wonder, spontaneous delight, or any experience that reveals the human spirit." -*e. e. cummings*

LIMITING BELIEFS

With infinite possibility
 we're born whole and complete
 pure and innocent.

As we learn to crawl and explore
 we soon hear "No, No, No"
 it's not OK to eat the cookie from the floor.

Our parents teach us how to act
 what's acceptable
 what's not
 having us think twice
 as we rub the welt
 from daddy's belt.

In the school years, we learn
 from our teachers and coaches
 told we are this, told we are that
 good at this, but not so good at that
 whiffing again with a baseball bat.

We learn from Church "virtue"

    from the law, limits of freedom

    from our peers, acceptance, or not

    and from them all

    duality of judgment.

The walls of the comfort box

    are fortified and

    reinforced against judgment

    A motionless, stagnant cell

    with nothing coming in nor going out.

Our comfort box is born

    of other's perceptions

    their limiting beliefs combined with

    our stories, our circumstances

    and our need to be right about them.

Suddenly we discover

    we have become

    the perceptions of others

    their limiting beliefs

    becoming our limiting beliefs.

The box is empty

except the baggage of the past

walls of protection against rejection.

What are you pretending not to know

asks the fox?

Who snickers and jumps the trap

of the comfort box.

And just then,

breaking through

the limiting beliefs

in the fire of my life,

standing there in the light of day,

it became clear

life begins outside the comfort box.

Dedicated to my brother Clark Smith who asked me to write on this subject, and Sylvia Badasci who first walked me through my own limiting beliefs.

"Most people are other people. Their thoughts are someone else's opinions, their lives a mimicry, their passions a quotation." *-Oscar Wilde*

GAINING ALTITUDE

Gaining altitude

    above life's journey

    above cyclic and painful emotion

    makes good sense to me

    when we rise above

    looking down upon

    Mother Earth, her beauty, her order.

Gaining altitude

    seeing perfectly plowed fields

    scattered towns

    city lights at night

    white puffy clouds

    the moonlight's reflection off

    the rolling sea.

Gaining altitude

    there is a certain order

    a certain perspective

    as we take vantage point

    from the creator's universal window

the earth a speck of light

and her humans' mere particles.

Gaining altitude

the view becomes clearer

how small and insignificant

we really are; particularly

in the need to be right about our stories,

limitations born of circumstance and

attachments to the past.

Gaining altitude

we elevate ourselves

above any drift

shifting unbearable pain into beauty

and releasing that which holds us back

we are free to fly high here

to be fully present in all our moments.

Dedicated to all those parents who have endured the loss of a child, and elevate themselves in the most powerful of ways under the worst of circumstance. I have come to know two such parents in my life. Theresa Whalin who lost her 17-year-old son Malloy Rodney Crabtree. Listening to Theresa's story and how she elevated herself and those around her was one of the most powerful conversations I have ever had. My friend Tiffany Harris lost her son Sullivan Mainor at age 9 years. Theresa and Tiffany's personal examples and elevations inspired this poem. This poem also remembers Malloy and Sullivan who were gone too soon. Theresa and Tiffany's choice to step into their power and to gain altitude over their situation was an example for us all, and led to this poem.

THE LAW OF ATTRACTION

Like attracts like

    Positive attracts positive

    The birthplace is simply feeling good

    Feeling good generates positive vibration

    Positive vibration radiates clear intention

    Clear intention creates our reality.

There is no condition or timeline on happiness

    Only you create your happiness, your joy

    It is already yours, take it

    and remain in gratitude

    Tell yourself I have versus I want.

The universe mirrors positive or negative thoughts

    So either way you're right!

Simply feeling good is most important

    feeling good is the source of what you attract

    You create the power of attraction

    for you are source of all

    What you seek; seeks you

What do you seek?

Call forth your reality

With an attitude of gratitude.

Be obedient to positive thoughts

We are already connected to everything we need

We already have everything we ever wanted

Visualize to materialize.

When you change, all else will change

Know you already have what you want

Be in gratitude for all you already have

You create the NOW

The universe creates the how

Ask, believe, receive, begins the creation.

For if the universe is a mirror for your thoughts

And you will receive back the positive or negative

Allow only positive thoughts

Allow and receive greatness, happiness

What are you manifesting?

What are you attracting?

We are born from the sea of infinite possibility,

and from that sea we create

Call forth your reality; your happiness, your joy,

The universe only says yes!

And so, you are right either way

whether positive or negative, you are right!!!!

Dedicated to my son Jake Smith who continues to learn to attract positive things.

CONSERVATION OF THOUGHT

What I'm for

    is far more important

    than what I'm against.

Focusing on what I'm for

    adds energy to that which I create.

    What you resist persists

    and focusing on things you are against

    adds energy to that resistance.

Why waste time adding to the negative energy

    of that which we are against?

Why not spend our time and energy creating what we

    are for?

Conservation of positive thought is what I'm for.

Dedicated to my son Trent who helped me write this while on a yellow tail fishing trip off San Clemente Island. We had had plenty of time to discuss politics and the tactics of a good debate in between calls of "Fish On!" Note: Trent, then 14 caught the biggest tuna on the boat, something he does regularly on our fishing trips.

Trent and I concluded that our politicians in Washington D.C. who run negative campaigns and spend more time speaking against other's political views versus the merits of their own views would well serve the nation if they spent their time speaking about what they are for vs. running negative campaigns. Why do they not speak for that which they are for?

THE CLIMB

Love

of life and nature scales upward

from the first faint awareness that something

of worth is there for absolute identification.

The lower and middle slopes of the scale

can be climbed by two or a team of many.

Not to gain the highest peak where you are

only here, and love of life and nature there and there,

but where all three become one, the same, indivisible.

The summit can only be reached alone

for the full absorption of each into the other

is a process as singular and as un-sharable as dying

or being born.

For it is he who conquers self that reaches the peak,

to discover a new valley

to begin the climb anew.

The way we climb is what matters most

for reaching any peak puts us in front

of yet another climb, another mountain.

Dedicated to my daughter Kiera, keep on climbing!

THE BALANCE

Out of nothing comes everything

Out of death comes life

Out of certainty comes possibility

Out of unattractiveness comes beauty

Out of dark, light

Out of hate, love

Out of lies, truth

Out of the vast stillness

A thought is born

A new frequency radiates

A new energy

The cycle repeats.

Balance, Balance in all things, Balance!

BLANK CANVAS

My blank canvas knows no past or future
    my blank canvas is the here and now
    my present moment
    shifting my energy to be present
    with all that is NOW.

My blank canvas questions what is possible
    in my present moment
    speaking to me with wise and kind words;
    "Project to the Universe all that you want on your
    blank canvas;
    for you are the source of all that you want."

My blank canvas is a manner of travel
    not a destination
    rather a journey, in search
    of what is possible in this moment.

When caught in my drift
    my blank canvas allows me to shift
    projecting onto the canvas

all that I source.

Where circumstance and excuse

begin to apply their toxic grip

my blank canvas erases all.

The blank canvas starts like all great inventions

from nothing a thought is born

a thought is a frequency

frequency is energy

Aye, we just created energy

with our thoughts.

The blank canvas asks,

"Do you accept that you are the creator of your

thoughts?"

My blank canvas makes me strong regardless of situation

resilient regardless of circumstance

by shifting negative energy into a positive place

and owning my power

to create a new positive picture

on my blank canvas.

My blank canvas acknowledges my past

    yet knows no limiting circumstance

    reflecting only that which is possible

    moment to moment.

The gift of the blank canvas is yours.

The blank canvas asks, "Why have it any other way."

Dedicated to my friend Jack Seri who introduced me to a blank

canvas.

THE VAST STILLNESS

Breathe into your body

    for you are alive.

    What do you want?

    What is your vision?

    All we have is this NOW!

    This moment to create possibility.

Breathe into your body

    for yesterday is gone.

    No sense living in our past.

    Who do you know

    that has a story

    that gives them permission

    to be right

    about their circumstance, their story

    trapping themselves in their past?

    Possibility does not live there.

Breathe into your body

    for life is urgent my friends.

It matters not what others may think

The man in the mirror

is the one we need to please

The man in mirror is also the only one

who can let us down.

What is the man in the mirror worth?

The reflection asks

So, what do you really, really want?

What is your vision?

The time is NOW!

Make haste,

for our final breath into the vast stillness awaits us all.

QUESTIONING DUALITY

For a thing to exist or be defined, must its opposite also exist?

> Must there be two halves to complete wholeness?

> Can there be a heaven without hell?

> Light without dark?

> God without Satan?

> Summer without winter?

> Pleasure without pain?

Why split the quality of one's choice into two categories of right or wrong?

Does reality lie between the questionable duality of right and wrong?

Do I live from mind (ego) consciousness or from soul (unity) consciousness?

Is there only one world, one people, one creation?

Wouldn't a shift from duality to nonjudgmental consciousness save energy and time, enabling a world that works?

QUESTION

Has there ever been a question on human relationships

    that could not be answered

    by unconditional love,

    forgiveness

    or compassion?

What was the question again?

Dedicated to my friend Robyn Williams, who I have heard say this many ways, many times.

WAKING THOUGHTS

I am grateful for this day
    I have everything I need
    to create anew
    to make a difference
    for those I love
    and for those I meet
Before the sunset carpe diem
Before the sunrise carpe diem
Forgiveness of others
    and more importantly of self
    is the blank canvas
    upon which I paint
    with a broader brush
    of possibility
    and a finer brush of intent
    the picture becomes clear
    the day is ours to create.

VULNERABILITY

What is your shame?

Where do you hide?

Addiction? Abuse? Un-worthiness?

Shame prevents human connection.

What makes you different?

What guilt? What shame?

Vulnerability is raw, naked

Expose shame, experience vulnerability.

What acceptance is missing?

What connection is missing?

Expose buried shame

Exit the dark cave.

Stand in bathing light of day

Come into light

Bask in its' warmth

Experience your experience.

Power comes from exposing shame

Suddenly there is nothing

Nothing to hide from

Nothing to come from.

Your greatest shame

Has become your greatest power

Moments in time released

The birthplace of power.

The shame forever released

No guarantee of acceptance

Other than self

The courageous stand revealed.

Dedicated to Brene Brown and her work to educate the world on vulnerability as power.

Author's Note on Emotional Intelligence

According to the Harvard Business Review (HBR), "Studies have shown that a high emotional quotient (or EQ) boosts career success, entrepreneurial potential, leadership talent, health, relationship satisfaction, humor, and happiness. It is also the best antidote to work stress and it matters in every job — because all jobs involve dealing with people, and people with higher EQ are more rewarding to deal with." HBR calls EQ the single most important determinant of success in life. Nearly 3,000 scientific articles have been published on EQ and a Harvard analysis of those reports found that a good coaching program can increase your EQ up to 50 percent. They also found that you can only improve if you get accurate feedback:

https://hbr.org/2013/05/can-you-really-improve-your-em

I went through EQ training at Choice Center Leadership University in Las Vegas, NV. I have seen so many positive results come out of the training both in my personal life, and in the lives of many others, that I am recommending the training for anyone reading this book.

The Choice Center curriculum is based on experiential learning. I like to say you experience your experience there. Like how you learned to ride a bike or swim, experiential learning lasts a lifetime. Very few of us can memorize a barrage of facts and retain all of them for a lifetime, but we remember our experiences. That's because experiential learning allows you to make discoveries and experiment with knowledge yourself instead of hearing or reading about the experiences of others. The outcome is the development of new skills, attitudes, behaviors, creative thinking, and ways of being that you adapt quickly and retain longer. Please check out Choice Center at:

https://www.choicecenter.com or shoot me an email at: blairsmith0505@gmail.com

SALIENT QUOTES

"It was when I found out I could make mistakes that I knew I was on to something." -*Ornette Coleman*

"Never let your head hang down. Never give up and sit down and grieve. Find another way. And don't pray when it rains if you don't pray when the sun shines." -*Satchel Paige*

"If you lack the iron and the fizz to take control of your own life, then the gods will repay your weakness by having a grin or two at your expense. Should you fail to pilot your own ship, don't be surprised at what inappropriate port you find yourself docked." -*Tom Robbins*

"No one can make you feel inferior without your consent." -*Eleanor Roosevelt, 1884-1962*

"Whoever battles with monsters had better see that it does not turn him into a monster. And if you gaze long into an abyss, the abyss will gaze back into you." -*Friedrich Nietzsche*

"Don't wait for the last judgment. It takes place every day." -*Albert Camus*

"The tragedy of life is what dies in the hearts and souls of people while they live." -*Albert Einstein*

"Learn to say no. It will be of more use to you than to be able to read Latin." -*Charles Haddon Spurgeon*

"Security is mostly a superstition. It does not exist in nature, nor do the children of men as a whole experience it. Avoiding danger is no safer in the long run than outright exposure. Life is either a daring adventure or nothing." -*Helen Keller*

"To dare to live alone is the rarest courage; since there are many who had rather meet their bitterest enemy in the field, than their own hearts in their closet." -*Charles Caleb Colton*

"Destiny is no matter of chance. It is a matter of choice: It is not a thing to be waited for, it is a thing to be achieved." -*William Jennings Bryan*

"Good leaders being scarce, following yourself is allowed." -*Anonymous*

"This life is a test. It is only a test. Had this been an actual life, you would have received further instructions as to what to do and where to go." -*Anonymous*

"Your life feels different on you, once you greet death and understand your heart's position." -*Louise Erdrich, Love Medicine (1984)*

"Do not be too timid and squeamish about your actions. All life is an experiment." -*Ralph Waldo Emerson*

"Don't say you don't have enough time. You have exactly the same number of hours per day that were given to Helen Keller, Louis Pasteur, Michelangelo, Mother Teresa, Leonardo DaVinci, Thomas Jefferson, and Albert Einstein." -*H. Jackson Brown, Jr.*

"Life is not lost by dying; life is lost minute by minute, day by dragging day, in all the thousand small uncaring ways." -*Stephen Vincent Benét*

"Don't ever become a pessimist...a pessimist is correct oftener than an optimist, but an optimist has more fun—and neither can stop the march of events." -*Robert A. Heinlein, Time Enough For Love, 1973*

"There are only two ways to live your life. One is as though nothing is a miracle. The other is as though everything is a miracle." -*Albert Einstein*

"Experience is what you get when you don't get what you want." -*Don Stanford*

"Words are the weak support of cold indifference; love has no language to be heard." -*William Congreve, The Double-Dealer (1694)*

"Whatever you do, or dream, begin it now... Boldness has genius, power and magic in it. Begin it now." -Goethe

"There are only two tragedies in life: one is not getting what one wants, and the other is getting it." -*Oscar Wilde*

"Reality is merely an illusion, albeit a very persistent one." -*Albert Einstein*

"The Universe has as many different centers as there are living beings in it." -*Alekswandr Solzhenitsyn*

"The surest way to corrupt a youth is to instruct him to hold in higher esteem those who think alike than those who think differently." -*Friedrich Nietzsche*

"Carpe diem, quam minimum credulapostero." Lat., "Seize the day, put no trust in tomorrow." -*Horace, Odes*

CHAPTER 2

HUMAN CERTAINTY

"The important thing is not to stop questioning" -*Albert Einstein*

"Believe those who are seeking the truth. Doubt those who find it." -*Andre Gide*

"This is my simple religion. There is no need for temples; no need for complicated philosophy. Our own brain, our own heart is our temple; the philosophy is kindness." -*Dalai Lama*

"In every country and every age, the priest has been hostile to Liberty." -*Thomas Jefferson*

"Somewhere, something incredible is waiting to be known." -*Carl Sagan*

"Human certainty ends the possibility of greater universal truths. I am for possibility and remain in question." -*Blair Smith*

CERTAINTY VERSUS THE FOX

Truth and certainty are strangers

    One certainty is strange to the other

    I am certain I am right, says

    The Catholic, The Muslim

    The Christian, The Jew

    The Capitalist, The Communist

    The Dictator, The Monarchy

Adolf Hitler, Joseph Stalin, Saddam Hussein,

Idi Amin Dada, Genghis Khan,

They were all certain too......

Man still goes to battle for as many proclaimed Gods

    as Gods that time has forgotten

    How many people have been killed

    In the name of religion?

    Of Governments and "Isms" past and present?

    Over the need to be "right"

    About something, anything

    How many more will be sacrificed?

Between the deep roots of man's certainties lie man's greatest battlefields.

One side convinced they are right,

and the other side equally insistent in their own

fundamental "righteousness"

Certainty ends possibility

why do we end what is possible?

Why does the human mind need to be certain?

For the truth is an old, old fox,

who has lived to be an old, old fox

by jumping the traps of human certainty.

Dedicated to all those who keep possibility alive by jumping the traps of human certainty and closed belief systems.

Postscript. The need to be right about our past, our circumstances, and our stories keeps us from being present to what is possible in this moment. Human certainty and the need to be right separates the great religions, and our nations.

WHY DO WE BELIEVE WHAT WE BELIEVE

Why do we believe what we believe?

What criteria does man use to validate beliefs?

How is information on man's beliefs gathered and measured?

How is this information subsequently analyzed, categorized and validated as "truth?"

What data management plan is used to validate human beliefs?

Or are we acting on faith versus validation?

So, how is God validated?

What set of criteria of any belief system proves the existence of any God?

How can we be so certain our beliefs are correct when they are not validated?

Certainty ends the possibility of being open to greater universal truth.

So, why do we believe what we believe?

And, what of the randomness of those beliefs?

Had we been born in England would we believe in Christianity?

Had we been born in Israel would we believe in Judaism?

Had we been born in Iran would we believe in Islam?

Had I been born anywhere else, would I simply take on the beliefs of my Fathers, who took on the beliefs of their Fathers?

And, what is the result of invalidated human belief?

Constant wars, with millions killed, mentally maimed and physically disfigured.

And, what are we to think of concentration camps holding the enemy, or internment camps filled with our own citizens?

So, what criteria do we use to validate human beliefs

Before we act with certainty?

The human mind will believe anything without validated proof

But once the mind has eaten one of 4,200 religions known today

The human mind is satisfied and moves on

Where it eats again, anything, usually without validation

Man's ultimate battlefield is played on the field of unvalidated human beliefs

Remember that the religious Zealot fiercely acts out his faith as well

And will continue to do so until he reaches infinity

Replete with nuclear bombs and terror

The religious Zealot's faith is not different than yours, or mine

An unvalidated belief, yet acted out with fierce conviction

And we question the Zealot's root to extremism?

Remember he acts upon his faith too.

One of the most important questions we can ask ourselves is "Why do I believe, what I believe?"

Unless we all better understand

Why we believe what we believe

We will continue to act on faith

Based on unvalidated information

Based on the past ways of our Fathers

Postscript: If what has been said here should shake any un-validated belief in any un-validated system then what has been said here has served its purpose.

Question to reader: So why do you believe, what you believe?

"Believe nothing, no matter where you read it, or who said it, no matter if I have said it, unless it agrees with your own reason and your own common sense."- *Buddha*

HUMAN BELIEF: THE DARK SIDE OF THE HUMAN MIND

Terrorists

Jim Jones

Inquisition

Nazi

Mass
Murders

Khomeini

Human
Bombs

Lynching

The Killing
Fields

Fanatic
Atheists

Holy Wars

Voodoo

Genocide

Hitler

9/11

Race
Superiority

Arab vs. Jew

Stalin

White Haters

Black Haters

The Holocaust

Pro-Life
Extremists

Pro-Abortion
Extremists

Fanatic
Republicans

Fanatic
Democrats

Christian
Fundamentalists

Moslem
Fundamentalists

Jewish
Fundamentalists

Human belief is an entity in itself
and like no other.

If held long enough, and deep enough,
and without question
the belief does not belong to the one who presumes
to possess it;
the believer belongs to the belief
and is ruled by it.

Such zealous conviction is hardier and more versatile
than any animate thing.

The belief thrives on wish as well as fact. For what the
belief wants to be true, claims to be true, and what is
true have become the same.

Wonder does not stunt its growth
for curiosity will not live beside it.

The belief can turn any scene
into what it wants the believer to see.

The belief can lead the feet
wherever it wants the believer to go
no matter the danger or reward.

The belief can digest all opposing facts
without so much as a belch,
for the belief's stomach has juices to turn all differing
views into food
that nourishes the one belief.

The belief has a thousand lives. The belief does not die
with the believer.
The belief lives on in the minds and the works of those
the Zealot has swayed.

THE CRUCIAL QUESTION

All questions fall into only a few categories:

> Who?
>
> What?
>
> When?
>
> Where?
>
> How?
>
> Why?

The only crucial question is "Why".

For, if the "why" is properly seen

> the "who's", "what's", "where's", "when's", and "how's"
>
> fall naturally into their proper places.

But if we are wrong on the big "WHY",

> we become no more than servants
>
> to our own mistake.

WHY do we believe, what we do believe?

> WHY are our convictions what they are?
>
> WHY do we not question the "WHY" of our own
>
> beliefs?

HOPE VERSUS THE ZEALOT

The Pentagon does not know the Zealot's name

    Or how to capture his determination

    Or how he might be found

    Or how to change his mind

    The Zealot is among us now

    No validation of fact versus myth

    No balance of reality versus dream

    No consciousness of good versus bad

    The Zealot's birthplace is hate

    His offspring hates even more

The Kamikazes

    The suicide bombers

    The rabid wolves of 9/11

    The scope of plans and results grow larger

    When the Zealot reaches infinity

    As no doubt he surely will

    Why build more bombs

    When more bridges are needed

The more determined Zealot is born

    He lies in wait

Deep in the hidden caverns of his mind

For more powerful explosives

For larger innocent targets

A faint shadow diminishing our birthrights

The forecast is kill or be killed

Survival of the fittest status quo

So, what is the Pentagon's budget for understanding

and compassion?

Could enlightened hope, just for once, be a plan

Are we hoping against hope?

NEW SCRIPTURE

In the library of the Universe

New Bible of possibility

Book of creation

Chapter of manifestation

Paragraph of thought

Verse of frequency

Sentence, particle-wave

It is written

"Destroy possibility and you destroy yourself."

Dedicated to my friend Robyn Williams, and to her work towards a world that works.

Postscript: If possibility were our "Scripture" anything would be possible despite any closed belief system. The problem with closed belief systems is that they close possibilities. Keep the possibility of greater universal truths alive!

SALIENT QUOTES

"It will yet be the proud boast of women that they never contributed a line to the Bible." -*George W. Foote*

"I have abandoned my search for truth, and am now looking for a good fantasy." -Ashleigh Brilliant

"We have just enough religion to make us hate, but not enough to make us love one another." -*Jonathan Swift, 1667-1745*

"The truth is that there is only one terminal dignity - love. And the story of a love is not important - what is important is that one is capable of love. It is perhaps the only glimpse we are permitted of eternity." -*Helen Hayes*

"To die for an idea is to set a rather high price on conjecture." -*Anatole France*

"The opposite of a correct statement is a false statement. The opposite of a profound truth may well be another profound truth." -*Niels Bohr (1885-1962)*

"Whenever you find yourself on the side of the majority, it is time to pause and reflect." -*Mark Twain*

"Christian: one who believes that the New Testament is a divinely inspired book admirably suited to the spiritual needs of his neighbors." -*Ambrose Bierce*

"A man's ethical behavior should be based effectually on sympathy, education, and social ties; no religious basis is necessary. Man would indeed be in a poor way if he had to be restrained by fear of punishment and hope of reward after death." -*Albert Einstein*

"If I am virtuous and worthy, for whom should I not maintain a proper concern?" -Confucius, Analects (6th C. B. C.)

"The total absence of humor from the Bible is one of the most singular things in all literature." -Alfred North Whitehead

CHAPTER 3

MANKIND

"We judge others by their actions; we judge ourselves by our intentions." *-Anonymous*

"You can only protect your liberties in this world by protecting the other man's freedom. You can only be free if I am free." *-Clarence Darrow (1857-1938)*

"The only thing necessary for the triumph of evil is for good men to do nothing." *-Edmund Burke (1729-1797)*

"Most of our suspicions of others are aroused by our knowledge of ourselves." *-Anonymous*

"It may be true that the law cannot make a man love me, but it can keep him from lynching me, and I think that is pretty important." *-Martin Luther King, Jr. (1929-1968)*

"Who are we? We find that we live on an insignificant planet of a humdrum star lost in a galaxy tucked away in some forgotten corner of a universe in which there are far more galaxies than people." *-Carl Sagan*

"Hence it comes about that all armed Prophets have been victorious, and all unarmed Prophets have been destroyed." *-Machiavelli the Prince, 1513*

I WONDER

Most of the time,

    I feel closer to that which is spiritual

    or closer to nature

    than to man

    and I am in gratitude.

Then sometimes, just sometimes,

    a rare human-to-human event unfolds

    to shed new light

    on the spirits

    of nature and man.

And then I wonder.

    Sometimes, just sometimes,

    I wish I could find cause

    to wonder more.

Dedicated to my friend Nancy Ruiz who wonders too.

"One of the most fashionable notions of our times is that social problems like poverty and oppression breed wars. Most wars, however, are started by well-fed people with time on their hands to dream up half-baked ideologies or grandiose ambitions, and to nurse real or imagined grievances." -*Thomas Sowell*

"Solemn history, I cannot be interested in...the quarrels of popes and kings, with wars and pestilences on every page,...and hardly any women at all." -*Jane Austen*

"I refuse to accept the view that mankind is so tragically bound to the starless midnight   of racism and war that the bright daybreak of peace and brotherhood can never become a reality... I believe that unarmed truth and unconditional love will have the final word." -*Martin Luther King, Jr.*

SKEWED RELATIVITY

People are nice

    but getting away on a fishing trip for a while

    is nicer.

After the while

    the fishing trip is nice

    but getting back with people again

    is nicer.

I spend more time fishing.

THE HUMAN MIND
(An Alien Graduate Student's Research Paper)

Human minds have led man's body to the moon

    and his machines to the stars.

But in his mind, there are still more Earth's that are flat

    than round.

There are still many suns circling

    many worlds.

The human mind has created a thousand more certainties

    than matters that are truly certain.

The human mind still allows more hate than understanding;

    more enemies than friends.

The human mind continues to lead man into battle

    for as many proclaimed Gods

    as Gods that time has forgotten.

And, man still knows less about his mind and his emotions

    than about what they produce.

Conclusion: the data reveals that the human mind remains largely untapped, and the potential, however small, is there for the human mind to capture its oneness with all that ever was and all that ever will be.

HOPE

Conviction so strong it dedicates a life

    with fanatic zeal

    has no allegiance to

    right or wrong

    fact or myth

    good or bad

    dream or reality.

Such belief listens only to spokesmen

    for unseen wants

    deep in the caverns

    of mind and emotion.

Now that the destructive arm of the Zealot

    can reach infinity

    the only hope for Mankind

    is that the secret voices will speak

    with more understanding and compassion

    than with prejudice and hate.

"We must accept finite disappointment, but never lose infinite
hope." -*Martin Luther King, Jr.*

COMMON DENOMINATOR

If the Universe has problems

    among the first must be

    to find a balance

    between stability and change.

This Earth itself has problems;

    few, if any, are larger

    than concern that humans

    will find the proper line

    between exploitation and conservation.

Additionally, human society has problems

    few, if any, are larger

    than finding the acceptable line

    between social order

    and individual freedom.

The individual human being has problems

    few, if any, are larger

    than finding the healthy line

    between motivating belief

    and searching skepticism.

Balance, balance-all is balance

Be stable but change

Use but conserve

Obey but be free

Believe but wonder

Balance, Balance —search for the balance!

THE TRUTH OF THE MATTTER

Why climb the mountain?

No!

Not because it is there;

because those below are everywhere!

CONDITIONED RESPONSE

If I had to chose

    between the Emperor of the Oaks

    and a human life

    I would kill the tree.

But my guilt would haunt me

    for the rest of my life

    and my shame would not let me rest.

MANKIND

I love mankind

    for the fine demonstrations

    he is capable of

    like human kindness, empathy,

    compassion, forgiveness,

    the ability to love

    and overcome adversity.

I love mankind

    for dreaming impossible dreams

    and making them happen;

    civil rights, men on the moon,

    radio, television

    the internet,

    and justice for ALL.

I love mankind

    when outwardly focused

    and being in service to his fellow man;

    like clean water in Africa projects,

    Doctors Without Boarders

and the United Nations

Children's Fund.

I love mankind daily

witnessing random acts of kindness

and hearing simple and honest words

like "I love you"

and experiencing community

including the homeless.

Yes, mankind is full of fine examples

of a higher spirit of human potential

leading me to the conclusion that

yes, I do love mankind,

It's people I can't stand!

MAN'S NATURE

High on dark stallions

Blue and Green Knights

Face off

Swords drawn

Death to one assured

The Blue Knight reflects

For peace to exist

Someone must go first

Maybe if I laid my sword down

The Green Knight would too

The Green Knight reflects

Without the Blue Knight

There are no questions

My ways would be right

Killing him would prove this

After all, survival of the fittest.

What does the Blue Knight pretend?

The observer reflects

What is man's true nature?

SALIENT QUOTES

"Hell is other people." -*Sartre*

"Man, as he is, is not a genuine article. He is an imitation of something, and a very bad imitation." -*P.D. Ouspensky, 1878-1947*

"All ambitions are lawful except those which climb upward on the miseries or credulities of mankind." -*Joseph Conrad, A Personal Record (1912)*

"Man would be otherwise. That is the essence of the specifically human." -*Antonio Machado, Juan de Mairena (1943)*

"After the great destructions / Everyone will prove that he was innocent." -Gunter Eich, Think of This (1955)

""The true measure of a man is how he treats someone who can do him absolutely no good." -*Ann Landers*

"We are ashamed of everything that is real about us; ashamed of ourselves, of our relatives, of our incomes, of our accents, of our opinions, of our experience, just as we are ashamed of our naked skins." -*George Bernard Shaw, Man and Superman*

"They are always saying God loves us. If that's love, I'd rather have a bit of kindness." -*Graham Greene, The Captain and the Enemy (1988)*

"I am sorry I offended you - I should have lied." -*Anonymous*

"Man is the only animal who causes pain to others with no other object than wanting to do so." -*Arthur Schopenhauer, 1788-1860*

"Everyone thinks of changing the world, but no one thinks of changing himself." -*Leo Tolstoi*

"O, what a tangled web we weave when first we practice to deceive!" -*Walter Scott*

CHAPTER 4

MOTHER EARTH

"Whatever befalls the earth befalls the sons of the earth"

-Chief Seattle

"Man did not weave the web of life, he is merely a strand in it. Whatever he does to the web, he does to himself."

-Chief Seattle

"The Whites too, shall pass-perhaps sooner than other tribes. Continue to contaminate your bed, and you will one night suffocate in your own waste"

-Chief Seattle

"Look deep into nature, and then you will understand everything better." *-Albert Einstein*

COMMENT FROM THE EARTH

Anything that has been here as long as the Earth
    should be able to tell us something.
    Is it this?
"You who have just come
    you who think I am yours alone
    you who have already caused my body to itch
    and twitch.
    You, too, shall pass away."

ABSURDITY

For a person or a nation to think

    that a piece of the Earth

    or its' water can be owned

    is absurd.

Forever may possess an instant

    but how can an instant own eternity?

The most to be claimed

    is a passing flash of stewardship.

LAMENT

There is no end to people who come

Nor to developers who build

There is no end to the land they want

    nor to what they will do

    to claim and change the open land

But there is an end to the first ground

    and we are almost there

As the old land goes

    more tap roots of the land

    and of the people who lived there

    are cut from the womb

The land and people both become

    faint and scattered shadows

    of what they were born to be

CHIEF SEATTLE SOUNDED WARNING

(Required Background Before Next Poem)

In 1855, Chief Seattle of the Washington Territory, Duwamish Tribe wrote a letter to then U.S. President, Franklin Pierce, in which he expressed his concern over the white man's concept of and attitude towards, Mother Earth.

Chief Seattle's poetic words, written long before ecology and conservation were thought about, came from the heart, and from intuitive love of the land, and all that it sustains:

"We know that the white man does not understand our way. One portion of the land is the same to him as the next, for he is a stranger who comes in the night and takes from the land whatever he needs. The earth is not his brother, but his enemy, and when he has conquered it, he moves on. He leaves his fathers' graves, and his children's birthright is forgotten. The sight of your cities pains the eye of the red man. But perhaps it is because the red man is a savage and does not understand."

"There is no quiet place in the white man's cities. The Indian prefers the soft sound of the wind darting over the face of the pond, and the smell of the wind itself cleansed by the mid-day rain or scented with a pinion pine. The air is precious to the red man. For all things share the same breath; the beasts, the trees, the man. The white man does not seem to notice the air he breaths. Like a dying man for many days, he is numb to the stench."

"What is a man without the beasts? If all the beasts were gone, men would die from great loneliness of spirit, for whatever happens to the beasts also happens to man. All things are connected. Whatever befalls the earth befalls the sons of earth."

"It matters little where we pass the rest of our days; they are not many. A few more hours, a few more winters, and none of the children of the great tribes that once lived on this earth, or that roamed in small bands in the woods, will be left to mourn the graves of people once as powerful and hopeful as yours."

"The whites too, shall pass - perhaps sooner than other tribes. Continue to contaminate your bed, and you will one night suffocate in your own waste. When the buffalo are all slaughtered, the wild horses all tamed, the secret corners of the forest heavy with the scent of many men, and the view of the ripe hills blotted by talking wires, where is the thicket? Gone. Where is the eagle? Gone. We might understand if we knew what it was the white man dreams, what hopes he describes to his children on the long winter nights, what visions he burns into their minds, so that they will wish for tomorrow. But we are savages. The white man's dreams are hidden from us."

Please proceed to the next poem Coffee with Chief Seattle.

Note: The City of Seattle, Washington is named after Chief Seattle.

COFFEE WITH CHIEF SEATTLE

You asked for my update on what the White Tribes dream; what visions and hopes they now pass on to their children. You say their dreams are hidden from you but they are not hidden from me, and I will tell you what they are, and what they are not.

They dream only of their own way,

> not of the next season,

> nor of the years of their children's children.

They dream of passing power and greed,

> not the lasting fruits of Mother Earth.

They dream of the greatness of their own possessions,

> not the greatness of their people.

They dream of their own wishes,

> not the wisdom of their wise men.

They dream of changing form and use of all they see;

> not a dream of hope that earth will endure unscathed.

They dream of what their minds can form,

> not of what their spirit can feel.

They dream of shiny trinkets, machines and structures;
not the beauty of the sunset.

However; Chief Seattle, your spirit may find some
consolation in this:

Increasingly, the children of the White Tribes do not
dream the dreams of their fathers.

More and more of them see wisdom in your words.

They too feel the loneliness of spirit of which you spoke;
they now begin to see what you meant by:

"Whatever befalls the Earth befalls the sons of Earth"

And, they are fighting the dreams of their ancestors that
ignore the womb from which all life is born.

Young people of now see more wisdom in your
words than seen by White Tribes of your day,
and they see your wisdom
growing in the opening minds
as the future becomes the present.

As you prophesied, man is beginning to suffocate under
his own waste.

But perhaps, just perhaps, enough children of all tribes

and countries, of all colors on Earth will

awaken to your warning before it's too late, and

turn back the tide of waste before

all surely drown.

Pray for us, Chief Seattle, that our dreams mirror the

Great Spirit.

THE CANYON TRAIL

Cathedrals, Palaces and Temples try

    to look

            like this

    to sound

            like this

    to touch

            like this.

    They can't.

BATHROOM MANNERS

Man's roads and highways

    splatter their excrement of

    billboards, buildings, factories,

    fences, water tanks and towns

    with less aesthetic care

    than is taken by a cat of the wilds,

    or a dog of the streets, when it picks the place

    to void its' bowels.

ONE DAWN ATOP HALEAKALA

They happened upon on me
 when I stood atop Haleakala
 10,000 feet above Maui's floor
 where the Silverswords grow.

Here in the House of the Sun,
 above the clouds below
 waiting those few precious moments
 for a new sun to rise.

Rising from the sea,
 through broken rain-clouds
 and across the sacred pink blanket,
 over the grey and white puffy clouds,
 the new sun begins to rise
 casting light across the expanding sky
 creating a warm light out of a cold night.

They spoke of this and they spoke of that.
 They spoke of the glories of nature
 and the blindness of those

who do not see her wonders.

Then, just as the last ray of the rising sun

rose from the sea and above the clouds,

warming rays were welcomed

by those withstanding cold

to see the beauty,

and they said:

"It is too beautiful for words, is it not?"

I walked away.

For it was just as they had said.

The morning was, indeed,

too beautiful for words.

GIGI'S SONG

The signs are everywhere

    In the air, we all breathe

    In the water, we all drink

    In the soil, we all grow our food

    In the land, we all live upon

    We are drowning in our own waste

    Global warming and climate change is here

    There is one Mother Earth and she is suffering

    mighty abuse

Over population, environmental degradation, famine

    Over fishing and over farming, poaching, starvation

Plastic waste everywhere even in the distant deep oceans

    Rising temperatures destroying crops

    Pollution, emissions, smog days, litter and waste

    Receding glaciers; half the rain forests gone

    Unsustainable use and destruction, greed over need

    And the population continues to grow

At this pace, there will be no tomorrows

    And few future generations of mankind

    Human actions are the root cause of all

Look at what we have done?

What will we do when the Earth dies?

The truth can be denied but not avoided

Can you blame Mother Earth for her reactions?

The very parent providing a home for all life

Within the scope of all

Is the ability to be earth friendly

There is still a chance

Enjoy but don't waste

Support clean energy

Use but conserve

Don't be a litter bug

Heal the planet one voice and one deed at a time!

Humanity's next great chapter

Is a change to higher consciousness

A change in thought

A change in environment

A widening of compassion

A new vision, A new way, A new planet

Embracing all mankind and together taking loving

care of everyone's home, Mother Earth

Starting with Reduce, Reuse and Recycle (R3)

We are the creators of Earth's evolution and healing

Together we will save Mother Earth

SEARCH

Perhaps, the sanest moments of my life have been a search

For nature as she was in the beginning-

the sights

the sounds

the smells

and the harmony of the silence.

Once I found such a place on a shelf of a mountain

and I would go there.

Houses grew in the distance

personifying septic boils

on the face of my Mona Lisa.

So, I found a place the houses could not follow

and I would go there.

Then, from the houses, the roads slithered out

biting the bosom of my Cleopatra.

So, I found another place roads could not go,

not their sight, sound, or smell

nor the sewage they bore.

And I would go there.

Then, the cancer of the roads ate outward

scarring the body of my new love.

The people walked the new trails there,

thinking voice alone to be discourse,

talking, shouting and laughing,

calling the stale crumbs of their taste

the loaf of freshness.

So, I found a hidden garden in the fold of a new mountain,

a haven no clothed creature will ever find

in my time.

There are no houses

no roads

no human trails-just the avenues of animals-

no taint of man.

So, I would go there. I am here and there now.

But a serpent has come to my Garden of Eden.

I cannot drive it away.

I cannot destroy it.

I cannot pull its' fangs.

Wherever I go it will be there before me.

It's the planes. The noise of the planes,

those smaller harsher ones

sweeping low to sense the earth,

as though the softness there

could pass through gloves of steel.

Violently they rape my last and only love.

Rhythms of the ages staggered with uncertainty

they seem confused.

They, too, do not know where to go.

The deer cannot hear the lion and is afraid.

Hide and seek for the fox and mouse has changed rules.

The mouth of the bird is open but no song comes forth.

The chuckling of the stream is drowned.

The earth shakes from these violations.

The trees tremble.

I weep.

I still go there.

There is no other place to go.

The planes are everywhere.

I go to the dismembered remains of nature

as she was in the beginning.

I go to the torn serenity as one who mourns for her.

"Sit still, very still and the universe will unfold before you, it has no choice." -*Franz Kafka*

THE ULTIMATE OBSCENITY

If I had to set out to do all one man can do

    To offend God-as-It-Lives-in-the-Wilderness

If I set out to do this in the most impious way

    A demonic mind can conceive,

I would not cut the trees and wash land away;

    There is an insult more blasphemous.

I would not kill the birds and animals;

    I can hurl a more sacrilegious taunt.

I would not foul the air and water there;

    I know a more vulgar curse.

What Satanic act could be more obscene than these?

Such wounds to the body might heal.

I would sear the vary soul of the vast stillness

    With maniacal shrieks of

    Cycle and boat,

    Snowmobile and plane.

SALIENT QUOTES

"We are in danger of destroying ourselves by our greed and stupidity. We cannot remain looking inwards at ourselves on a small and increasingly polluted and overcrowded planet."
-Stephen Hawking

"Sooner or later, we will have to recognize that the Earth has rights, too, to live without pollution. What mankind must know is that human beings cannot live without Mother Earth, but the planet can live without humans." *-Evo Morales*

"My soul can find no staircase to Heaven unless it be through Earth's loveliness." *-Michelangelo*

"The question before the human race is, whether the God of nature shall govern the world by his own laws, or whether priests and kings shall rule it by fictitious miracles."
-John Adams

"The earth is the mother of all people, and all people should have equal rights upon it." *-Chief Joseph*

"The Earth does not belong to us: we belong to the Earth."
-Marlee Matlin

"The earth laughs in flowers." *-e.e. cummings*

"We all should plant some trees we'll never sit under."
-Anonymous

"What nature requires is obtainable, and within easy reach. It's for the superfluous we sweat."
-Seneca, Letters ToLucilius (1st C.)

"Infuse your life with action. Don't wait for it to happen. Make it happen. Make your own future. Make your own hope. Make your own love. And whatever your beliefs, honor your creator, not by passively waiting for grace to come down from upon high, but by doing what you can to make grace happen… yourself, right now, right down here on Earth."
-Bradley Whitford

"Once you've been in space, you appreciate how small and fragile the Earth is." -Valentina Tereshkova

"Life is abundant, and life is beautiful. And it's a good place that we're all in, you know, on this earth, if we take care of it."
-Alice Walker

"I believe alien life is quite common in the universe, although intelligent life is less so. Some say it has yet to appear on planet Earth." -Stephen Hawking

CHAPTER 5

THE CREATIVE POEMS

"There is no reality except the one contained within us. That is why so many people live such an unreal life. They take the images outside them for reality and never allow the world within to assert itself." -*Hermann Hesse, Demian (1919)*

"To laugh often and much; to win the respect of intelligent people and the affection of children; to earn the appreciation of honest critics and endure the betrayal of false friends; to appreciate beauty, to find the best in others; to leave the world a little better; whether by a healthy child, a garden patch or a redeemed social condition; to know even one life has breathed easier because you have lived. This is the meaning of success."
-Ralph Waldo Emerson

"It has been my experience that folks who have no vices have very few virtues." -*Abraham Lincoln , 1809-1865*

"I love to see a young girl go out and grab the world by the lapels. Life's a bitch. You've got to go out and kick ass."
-Maya Angelou

"I am ready to meet my Maker. Whether my Maker is prepared for the great ordeal of meeting me is another matter."
-Winston Churchill

"I know reincarnation is a fact…it had to take me more than one lifetime to get this fucked up." -*Swami X*

"Hell, there are no rules here--we're trying to accomplish something." -*Thomas A. Edison*

"Darkness cannot drive out darkness; only light can do that. Hate cannot drive out hate; only love can do that."
-*Martin Luther King, Jr.*

"Injustice anywhere is a threat to justice everywhere."
-*Martin Luther King, Jr.*

"The highest levels of performance come to people who are centered, intuitive, creative, and reflective - people who know to see a problem as an opportunity."
-*Deepak Chopra*

"I would define, in brief, the poetry of words as the rhythmical creation of Beauty." -*Edgar Allan Poe*

While I know myself as a creation of God, I am also obligated to realize and remember that everyone else and everything else are also God's creation." -*Maya Angelou*

THE RIVER SOUL

Where does the river lead?

    Where does it flow?

    Will it join other rivers,

    or simply empty into the sea?

    Will it swallow me,

    or lead me to my destination?

    Sometimes it doesn't matter

    if anywhere is better than where you are.

Trust and cross the soul of the river and you will become:

    A ray of the sun

    A drop of the rain

    A wisp of the wind

    A wave of the ocean

    A grain of the sands

    A bark of the great oak

Where brooks and streams babble, may I hear your voice.

Where eagles soar, may I be feathers on your wing.

Mynea went there too by crossing the river in body and spirit

and was born again by becoming one with all there ever was,

and all that ever will be.

Note: This poem was written through the voice of a little Hmong girl whom I named Mynea. While standing on the bank of the Laos side of the Mekong River, Mynea is too afraid to cross as she does not know how to swim, however staying on the Communist side of Laos was not an option. Freedom beacons across the Mekong.

Mynea's father, a Hmong officer, was killed for supporting the United States during the Silent War, but still watches over her in spirit, offering love, encouragement and empowerment in the only way now possible. Mynea reminds us all that we are born again by facing our fears and crossing our own river soul.

Author's Note: This poem is my personal favorite as it evokes the most emotion in me. My eyes well up just looking at it knowing how much it meant to me and how deep I had to go to become Mynea and her Father.

Dedicated to the Hmong people and all refugees who crossed the Mekong River into Thailand escaping the revenge of Communist Laos and Communist Viet Nam.

Background Reading on Operation Babylift

With the Viet Nam War coming to an imminent end, on April 3, 1975, U.S. President Gerald Ford announced that the U.S. Government would begin evacuating orphans from Saigon in a series of 30 planned flights aboard Military Airlift Command (MAC) C-5A Galaxy and C-141 Starlifter cargo aircraft. The plan would be known as Operation Babylift. Over 2,500 children were relocated and adopted by families in the United States and by her allies. Operation Babylift might well be the only thing the United States did right during the Viet Nam War. Many great service organizations and individuals were involved in this massive humanitarian effort. As much as I would like to acknowledge everyone involved, this poem is dedicated to my friend United States Air Force Captain Robert "Coach" Cunningham who would make three round trips across the Pacific in his C-141 Starlifter to bring over 240 orphan babies to new to beginnings. In the following picture, "Coach" is seen aboard his C-141 Starlifter on forward left side holding one of the orphan babies.

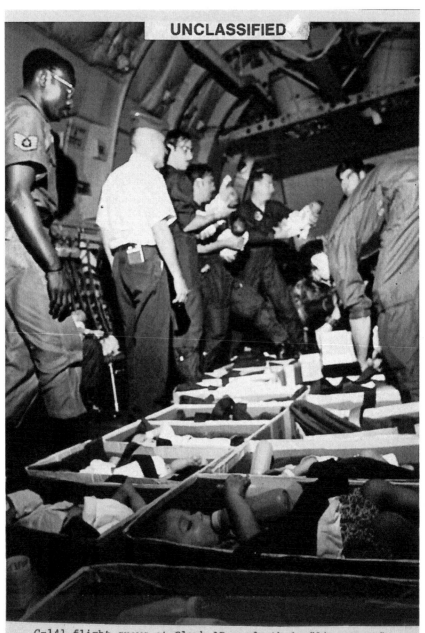

C-141 flight crews at Clark AB ready their "live cargo" for the journey.

132

OPERATION BABYLIFT

As America abandoned a land far away
In a war of broken agreements
There is one thing, just one, that made sense
Keeping a final word
Of a great humanitarian effort
Operation Babylift was born

To Captain Robert "Coach" Cunningham
Operation Babylift called his name
Aboard his C-141Starlifter
"A transformed flying womb"
Across the Pacific
With 240 orphan babies

An orphan's story began
As a toxic war was ending
New families
New beginnings
Cultural roots and
Identity lost and found in time

No more agent orange mission today
Babies away vs. bombs away
At least for now
A melody of tears
Accompanies the memory
"Kam ung" Coach, "Kam ung"

Note: "Kam ung" means thank you in Vietnamese language.

Dedicated to my friend Robert "Coach" Cunningham who made three round trips across the Pacific carrying a total of 240 babies to America.

CRITERION

How can the value of an opinion be measured?

The major measure of ignorance, or of subterfuge

    in both politics and religion

    is that the links between cause and effect

    are said to be evident, few, and simple.

The major measure of the wisdom of opinion

    is that the possessor,

    while standing firm when necessary,

    is still searching.

BIRD WORDS

Words for the shrieking Bluejays

    who scold the modest Sparrow and Thrush:

"Brilliance and sophisticated sentences

    seem to go quite well

    with one other.

But large words and wisdom

    are seldom found together."

OMAR SPEAKS AGAIN

When you take thy loaf of bread

    Thy sip of wine,

    And thy self-beside you

    Into the desert of wonderment

    'Tis not enow

Ye must bring back the empty jug!

Dedicated to my Father Dennis Smith who bought The RUBAIYAT of OMAR KHAYYAM for me on Christmas realizing I was going to drink from the same jug!

MODERN TRESPASSING

The modern trespassers are EVERYWHERE

> spawning pandemic virus

> without respect for privacy

> and certainly without invitation.

The modern trespassers spread their virus

> in the excrement of that from which they profit

> on my property, in my mailbox

> in my phone, my internet,

> my computers and my radios.

The virus is everywhere and absolutely relentless.

> The modern trespassers rob me of my peace,

> And to all of them,

> I say again

No, my warranty is not expiring

> and No I don't need a new loan.......you bastards

No, I did not make an inquiry for new life insurance

> and No I was not randomly selected for a

> vacation.......you bastards

And no, I did not win a cruise

> within your floating prison

from which you profit.......you bastards.

The virus compromises my personal data

as it Phishs, scams, and steals identity.

The modern trespassing virus poisons my vision

with billboards of sight pollution

and affects my hearing,

spewing vomit of propaganda.

Our privacy and possessions

are the viral hunting grounds.

The bombardment has left most numb

as though the virus is the norm.

I'm for laws against these intentional torts.

DON'T TREAD ON ME

YOU MODERN TRESPASSING BASTARDS

Survivors will be prosecuted!

THE FACE OF PRIDE

Pride is my friend

    Thoughts of satisfaction, fulfillment

    Feelings of elevated joy

    In jobs well done

    Triumph over personal adversity

    A byproduct of praise

Black pride, Asian pride

    LGBTQ pride, White pride

    Team pride, Organization pride

    Bringing each group identity

    Fulfilling needs to belong

Pride is found in many ways

    Achieving lofty goals

    Taking a stand

    Passing the test

    Finishing the race

Pride is found in

    Organizations contributing to community

    Attachment to groups

    Attachment to culture, family

Fulfilling many needs, but

Pride is my enemy

    Pride is self-serving

    Thinking I am Superior

    To my neighbor and

    Better than anyone else

Nations taking false pride

    Whose offspring is war

    Leading to injury or death

    False pride on one side

    False pride on the other side

    Families separated, innocence destroyed

Individuals taking false pride

    Whose offspring is superiority

    Leading to judgment of the less fortunate

    Self-congratulatory pride

    Boasts, brags and gloats

    Thoughtlessly applied to self

In the greatest story ever told

    Satan was proud

    To take the place of God himself

    And was sent to Hell for such pride

Pride is both friend and enemy

Pride is best served with a double dose of humility

"It was pride that changed angels into devils; it is humility that makes men as angels." -*Saint Augustine*

"Anger is the enemy of non-violence and pride is a monster that swallows it up." -*Mahatma Gandhi*

"Generosity is giving more than you can, and pride is taking less than you need." -*Khalil Gibran*

"There are two kinds of pride, both good and bad. 'Good pride' represents our dignity and self-respect. 'Bad pride' is the deadly sin of superiority that reeks of conceit and arrogance."
-*John C. Maxwell*

"Pride is the last thing a good man gets rid of."
-*Edmund Burke*

"Remembering that I'll be dead soon is the most important tool I've ever encountered to help me make the big choices in life. Because almost everything - all external expectations, all pride, all fear of embarrassment or failure - these things just fall away in the face of death, leaving only what is truly important." -*Steve Jobs*

A PUZZLE SOLVED

Which comes first, the cause or the advocate?

Does the cause produce the advocate,

or does the advocate produce the cause?

So which is chicken, and which is egg?

The answer must lie in the needs of the two:

The need of the cause is singular,

only one response can meet it.

The needs of the advocate are many and can be met

by any one of a thousand causes.

The needs of the cause are clear and easily seen.

The needs of the advocate are mixed and murky;

rarely clearly sensed,

but strongly defined as one thing

when they are usually another.

There is a need for a cause

or the advocate would not have found it.

The need of the advocate is a magnet;

drawing to it any cause that is palatable to its taste.

So the advocate (in this case the chicken) comes first;
It seeks until it finds a cause (in this case an egg)
and gives nest as if it if it were its own and new
though hens of history laid the egg long ago.

THE MIRROR

What I see in you

   I see in me

   I see our good

   And I see our holes

My judgment of you

   Is judgment of myself

   For the mirror reflects all

   Sparing none

What would we look like

   if all mankind

   looked in the mirror

   at once?

"When I speak to you about myself, I am speaking to you about
yourself. How is it you don't see that?"
-Victor Hugo

"We don't see things as they are, we see things as we are."
-Anais Nin

I AM

I command, I AM

    I am who and what

    I say I AM

    Letting go of negative belief

    As a matter of choice

    "I AM", I said

    I AM whole

    I AM abundance

    I AM worthy

    I AM success

    I AM grateful

    I AM connected

Conservation of thought

On the positive I AM

Affirming what I AM

Attracting what I AM

Reflecting the very Great Spirit

We were all born to be

Dedicated to all my foster brothers and sisters who may need a few words of empowerment and a reminder that we get to choose how we let all of our experiences (including foster care) define us. This is poem is further dedicated to Natalia Yungerlevi my foster sister, Mila Dunn my foster youth I was a Court Appointed Special Advocate (CASA) for, and Sabrina Goosby the Vice President of Voices for Children San Diego who has dedicated her professional life to helping foster youth.

SALIENT QUOTES

"Reality is that which, when you stop believing in it, doesn't go away." *-Phillip K. Dick, 1928-1982*

"In the beginning the Universe was created. This has made a lot of people very angry and been widely regarded as a bad move." *-Douglas Adams*

"What is hateful to you do not do to your neighbor. That is the whole Torah. The rest is commentary." *-Hillel (30 B.C.-A.D. 10)*

"The gods too are fond of a joke." *-Aristotle (384-322 B.C.)*

"Most people are bothered by those passages of Scripture they do not understand, but the passages that bother me are those I do understand." *-Mark Twain*

"Whatever women do they must do twice as well as men to be thought half as good. Luckily, this is not difficult." *-Charlotte Whitton*

"It is well to remember that the entire population of the universe, with one trifling exception, is composed of others." *-Andrew J. Holmes, 1946*

"Appearances are not held to be a clue to the truth. But we seem to have no other." *-Dame Compton-Burnett, 1884-1969*

"I wish to report the strange disappearance of my hopes and dreams." *-Ashleigh Brilliant*

"There are moments when everything goes well; don't be frightened, it won't last." *-Jules Renard*

"The absolute yearning of one human body for another particular body and its indifference to substitutes is one of life's major mysteries." *-Iris Murdoch*

"No woman ever falls in love with a man unless she has a better opinion of him than he deserves." *Edward W. Howe*

"And those who were seen dancing were thought to be insane by those who could not hear the music." *Friedrich Nietzsche*

"Destiny is no matter of chance. It is a matter of choice: It is not a thing to be waited for, it is a thing to be achieved."
William Jennings Bryan

"The belief in a supernatural source of evil is not necessary; men alone are quite capable of every wickedness."
-Joseph Conrad, 1857-1924

"Children today are tyrants. They contradict their parents, gobble their food, and tyrannize their teachers."
-Plato - The Republic

"We receive three educations, one from our parents, one from our schoolmasters, and one from the world. The third contradicts all that the first two teach us."
-Baron de Montesquieu 1689-1750

"It may be that your whole purpose in life is simply to serve as a warning to others." *-Anonymous*

"The only reason for time is so that everything doesn't happen at once." *-Albert Einstein*

"To knock a thing down, especially if it is cocked at an arrogant angle, is a deep delight to the blood."
-George Santayana, The Life of Reason (1903)

"We have enslaved the rest of the animal creation, and have treated our distant cousins in fur and feathers so badly that beyond doubt, if they were able to formulate a religion, they would depict the Devil in human form."
-*William Ralph Inge, Outspoken Essays (1922)*

"If you think no one cares you're alive, try missing a couple of car payments." -*Anonymous*

"I have not been afraid of excess: Excess on occasion is exhilarating. It prevents moderation from acquiring the deadening effect of a habit." *Somerset Maugham*

"You have to stay in shape. My grandmother, she started walking five miles a day when she was 60. She's 97 today and we don't know where the hell she is." -*Ellen DeGeneres*

"All of the animals except man know that the principal business of life is to enjoy it." -*Samuel Butler*

"A woman drove me to drink and I didn't even have the decency to thank her." -*W. C. Fields*

"For most of history, Anonymous was a woman."
-*Virginia Woolf*

"I owed the government $3400 in taxes. So I sent them two hammers and a toilet seat." -*Michael McShane*

"Among those whom I like or admire, I can find no common denominator, but among those whom I love, I can: all of them make me laugh."
W. H. Auden, The Dyer's Hand

"Jesus loves you, but everyone else thinks you're an asshole."
-*Anonymous*

"If Patrick Henry thought that taxation without representation was bad, he should see how bad it is with representation."
-*Old Farmer's Almanac, 1881*

"The function of the law is not to provide justice or to preserve freedom. The function of the law is to keep those who hold power, in power."
-*Gerry Spence, From Freedom to Slavery, 1993*

"Women and Cats will do as they please. Men and Dogs had better get used to it."
-*Robert Heinlein, Time Enough for Love*

"Events are less important than our response to them."
-*Anonymous*

"Be careful of your thoughts, they may become words at any moment." -*Anonymous*

"Be tender to the young, compassionate to the aged, tolerant with the weak. For in your life you will be all of these."
-*Anonymous*

"No bird soars too high if he soars with his own wings."
-*William Blake*

"We are the miracle of force and matter making itself over into imagination and will. Incredible. The Life Force experimenting with forms. You for one. Me for another. The Universe has shouted itself alive. We are one of the shouts."
-*Ray Bradbury, "G.B.S. - Mark V"*

"In the little world in which children have their existence, whosoever brings them up, there is nothing so finely perceived and so finely felt, as injustice."
-*Charles Dickens, Great Expectations (1860)*

"To make the child in your own image is a capital crime, for your image is not worth repeating. The child knows this and you know it. Consequently you hate each other."
-*Karl Shapiro, The Bourgeois Poet (1964)*

AFTERTHOUGHT

As noted in the forward, I first intended the "the poems" just for my Grandkids and Great-Grandkids in case I never got to meet or know them. To them I also say, I wanted to leave you something more than a scattered picture of a smile left behind. My "WHY" was to connect with you, to speak with you, to touch you in some way, so you would know I was here. Along the way, I connected with many others by sharing with them what was originally meant for you. So thank you for being that inspiration.

Beyonce Knowles Lyrics

"I Was Here"

(Excerpt)

I wanna leave my footprints on the sands of time

Know there was something that, meant something that I left

behind

When I leave this world, I'll leave no regrets

Leave something to remember, so they won't forget

I was here

I lived, I loved

I was here

I did, I've done everything that I wanted
And it was more than I thought it would be
I will leave my mark so everyone will know
I was here

I wanna say I lived each day, until I die
And know that I meant something in somebody's life
The hearts I have touched will be the proof that I leave
That I made a difference, and this world will see

I was here
I lived, I loved
I was here
I did, I've done everything that I wanted
And it was more than I thought it would be
I will leave my mark so everyone will know

I was here

ABOUT THE AUTHOR
-Blair Smith-

Blair has worn, and continues to wear, many hats. Retired as a Navy pilot at the early age of 39, Delta Air Line pilot (until the events of 9/11), on staff with Booz Allen Hamilton for two years assigned to operational tests and experimentation in support of the Navy's Space and Naval Warfare Systems (SPAWAR), followed by 11 years as program manager for General Atomics (GA), leading a civilian team of 280 patriots supporting the US Air Force's Global War on Terrorism (GWOT) with MQ-9 Reaper and MQ-1 Predator operations.

Blair holds a Master's Degree in Organization Development from the University of San Francisco, additionally completing the U.S. Navy's Post Graduate

School Curriculum in Monterrey, CA, leading to his designation as an Aviation Safety Officer. He remains a licensed Federal Aviation Administration (FAA) Airline Transport Pilot (ATP) and Turbojet Flight Engineer (FE), having logged over 5,000 flight hours while qualifying in Jets, Props and Helicopters.

Concurrently, Blair is an Associate Professor at Embry-Riddle Aeronautical University where he has taught over 100 undergraduate and graduate courses, both online and in the classroom. He continues to teach part time as a labor of love.

In the community, Blair is on the Board of Blank Canvas Youth, a non-profit organization dedicated to providing transitional housing and general educational services, emphasizing independent living skills for foster youth. Blair is himself a former foster youth and knows full well both the agony and the pitfalls attendant to foster care. It is his mission to improve the lives of all foster youth, past, present and future. To that end, he has also served as a Court Appointed Special Advocate (CASA) for troubled fosters.

As of this writing, Blair and his family reside in Las Vegas, NV where he is presently employed by the Nevada Institute for Autonomous Systems (NAIS). His designation is Senior Program Manager and his duties include close support of the efforts of NASA and the FAA in the development of the Unmanned Traffic Management (UTM) System leading to the safe integration of drones into the National Airspace (NAS).

ACKNOWLEDGEMENTS

I would like to take this opportunity to acknowledge my entire family. First, my beautiful and dedicated wife Pranee for her total support and to my super kids Kiera, Jake, and Trent who understood my time doing this was just me being me. Special thanks to my brother Clark for walking this journey with me from step one. Clark always made himself available to proof this work even at the oddest hours just to give me feedback when I was working on a poem. And to my father, Dennis, who gave me life, and the opportunity to become a larger person than who I had been. My chief editors, Dennis, and Clark kept me straight and provided the guiding feedback required to produce this book. Denna Atkinson also contributed to the editing process. Also, a big thank you to my coach Mike Bruely who is always full of encouragement and understanding, and, who always keeps my best interests in mind. Mike knows the song in my heart and sings it back to me when I forget. A special thanks to Ray Brennan and Lowell Ellis, my Aviation Officer Candidate School classmates and brothers from class "10-90 marching into chow" for the encouragement along the way. Tela Holcomb is credited for taking a stand for me as "my angel". Karen "Homie K" Brasch also gets a big shout out for being an early on reviewer and supporter. Leslie Sullivan is credited for providing the pictures and conversions to black and white. A final shout out to Alectra Edison and Curt Kouser who took care of me at every turn.

A heartfelt thank you to Dr. Gloria Bader who walked me through Graduate school as my mentor. She watched and encouraged me to evolve from a young enlisted man earning his Master's degree into a Naval Aviator, and now to "giving birth" (Gloria's words) to *The Poems*.

Finally, to the man who has influenced my thinking and way of "Being" the most, Dr. Carlos Efferson (my Great Uncle by marriage) for showing me the greatest kindness I have ever known. The true quality times aboard his good ship Jubilo fishing for Sturgeon in San Francisco Bay, our talks in his special cabin and our hikes in the hills of Las Trampas are all passed forward in these poems.

And to you my readers "Namaste" the divine in me, bows to the divine in you. Be kind to yourself, your body, and to others without judgments.

"My rock, Pranee Smith, who always has my back."

"My favorite fly fisherman, Jake and Trent near Provo, Utah.
#Ispendmoretimefishing!!"

"The Haul! Two great fisherman, Jake and Trent off Seward, Alaska."

"King Salmon fishing the Kenai River, Alaska. Trent AKA "T$" lands the biggest king salmon of the day."

"The kids, Kiera, Jake and Trent on family vacation to Maui."

"Me and brothers Brett and Clark sharing a round of cheer. #RIP brother Brett in your mountain home."

"Grandma Jeannie age 95, getting excited over her bag of "goodies!"

My brother Clark and his two boys (my nephews) Kyle and Tyler."

"My daughter Kiera living the dance life."

"My dad Dennis age 77 years with Trent. Trent had just won the Nevada State championship for middle school boys in wrestling at 106lbs."

"My brother Clark with his partner Stephanie."

"Those were the days my friends. I never wanted them to end. Such fond memories I am blessed with. Picture taken aboard USS Carl Vinson somewhere in the middle of the Pacific Ocean."

"Dr. Carlos Efferson (My Great Uncle by Marriage) taking Clark and I fishing in San Francisco Bay. I was around 13-14 years old in this picture."

"My dad with daughter Kiera."

"My Delta Air Lines days living in Reno, NV."

"Jake with a nice Rainbow Trout for dinner! Fly fishing near Provo, Utah."

"Jake and I landing some nice Halibut off Homer, Alaska. Jake won this day with a 64 pounder!"

"Silver salmon for dinner somewhere in remote Alaska."

"Date night some years ago! Who knew!!"

AVAILABILITY

Blair has gained great insight into the human condition and, moreover, is a skilled speaker/communicator with a demonstrated ability to understand and motivate others. He is available for speaking engagements within a variety of venues, particularly on the topics of "the poems" and anything related to foster youth.

Contact information is as follows:
blairsmith0505@gmail.com.

ELEGY

Note to the reader: Fill in the blank spaces below when the information becomes available

On the day of August 16th of the year 2018

At age 57, it was recorded here that his spirit joined these poems

On this date _____of the year _____ at age _____

his body went there too,

where he had become altogether

present with all that has ever been and all that shall ever be

he had taken his final breath into the vast stillness

and was born again.

Made in the USA
San Bernardino, CA
19 January 2019